# Starting with... Role play

## Fairy tales

Diana Bentley

Maggie Hutchings

Dee Reid

Diana Bentley is an educational consultant for primary literacy and has written extensively for both teachers and children. She worked for many years in the Centre for the Teaching of Reading at Reading University and then became a Senior Lecturer in Primary English at Oxford Brookes University. Throughout her professional life she has continued to work in schools and teach children aged from 5 to 11 years.

Maggie Hutchings has considerable experience teaching KS1 and Early Years. She is a Leading Teacher for literacy in The Foundation Stage and is a Foundation Stage and Art coordinator. Maggie is passionate about the importance of learning through play and that learning should be an exciting and fun experience for young children. Her school's art work has been exhibited in The National Gallery, London.

Dee Reid is a former teacher who has been an independent consultant in primary literacy for over 20 years in many local authorities. She is consultant to 'Catch Up' – a special needs literacy intervention programme used in over 4,000 schools in the UK. She is Series Consultant to 'Storyworlds' (Heinemann) and her recent publications include 'Think About It' (Nelson Thornes) and Literacy World (Heinemann).

Other titles in the series:

Colour and light
Under the ground
Emergency 999
Into space
At the shops
Fairytales
At the garage/At the airport
All creatures great and small
On the farm
Water
Ourselves

Other Foundation titles:

Starting with stories and poems:

Self esteem
Self care
A sense of community
Making relationships
Behaviour and self control

A collection of stories and poems

Starting with our bodies and movement

Starting with sounds and letters

---

The authors would like to thank Jane Whitwell for all her hard work in compiling the resources and poems for the series.

---

Published by
Hopscotch Educational Publishing Ltd, Unit 2, The Old Brushworks, 56 Pickwick Road, Corsham, Wiltshire, SN13 9BX
Tel: 01249 701701

© 2006 Hopscotch Educational Publishing

Written by Diana Bentley, Maggie Hutchings and Dee Reid
Series design by Blade Communications
Cover illustration by Sami Sweeten
Illustrated by Nick Raybould
Printed by Colorman (Ireland) Ltd

ISBN 1 905390 17 3

Diana Bentley, Maggie Hutchings and Dee Reid hereby assert their moral right to be identified as the authors of this work in accordance with the Copyright, Designs and Patents Act, 1988.

The authors and publisher would like to thank Chapter One (a specialist children's bookshop) in Wokingham for all their help and support. Email: chapteronebookshop@yahoo.co.uk

All rights reserved. This book is sold subject to the condition that it shall not, by way of trade or otherwise, be lent, hired out or otherwise circulated without the publisher's prior consent in any form of binding or cover other than that in which it is published and without a similar condition, including this condition, being imposed upon the subsequent purchaser.

No part of this publication may be reproduced, stored in a retrieval system, or transmitted, in any form or by any means, electronic, mechanical, photocopying, recording or otherwise, without the prior permission of the publisher, except where photocopying for educational purposes within the school or other educational establishment that has purchased this book is expressly permitted in the text.

# Contents

| | |
|---|---|
| Introduction | 4 |
| 'Fairy tales' planning chart | 6 |
| Week 1 – Cottage and castle | 7 |
| Week 2 – Cottage equipment | 12 |
| Week 3 – Jack's cottage | 16 |
| Week 4 – Harps, hens and coins! | 20 |
| Week 5 – The fairytale castle | 24 |
| Week 6 – The banquet | 28 |
| Photocopiables | 31 |

**Acknowledgements**

The authors and publisher gratefully acknowledge permission to reproduce copyright material in this book.

'The digging song' by Wes Magee. © Wes Magee. Reproduced by kind permission of the author.
'A bedtime rhyme for young fairies' and 'The new fairy godmother' by Clare Bevan. © Clare Bevan. First published by Macmillan. Reproduced by kind permission of the author.
'Giant's breakfast' by Judith Nicholls. © Judith Nicholls. Reproduced by kind permission of the author.
'I'd be a good friend' from The Bees Knees by Roger McGough (Copyright © Roger McGough, 2003) is reproduced by permission of PFD (www.pfd.co.uk) on behalf of Roger McGough.

Every effort has been made to trace the owners of copyright of material in this book and the publisher apologises for any inadvertent omissions. Any persons claiming copyright for any material should contact the publisher who will be happy to pay the permission fees agreed between them and who will amend the information in this book on any subsequent reprint.

# Introduction

There are 12 books in the series *Starting with role play* offering a complete curriculum for the Early Years.

| | |
|---|---|
| Ourselves | At the garage/At the airport |
| Into space | Emergency 999 |
| At the shops | All creatures great and small |
| Colour and light | Under the ground |
| At the hospital | Fairytales |
| On the farm | Water |

While each topic is presented as a six-week unit of work, it can easily be adapted to run for fewer weeks if necessary. The themes have been carefully selected to appeal to boys and girls and to a range of cultural groups.

 Each unit addresses all six areas of learning outlined in the *Curriculum Guidance for the Foundation Stage* and the specific Early Learning Goal is identified for each activity and indicated by this symbol.

Generally, differentiation is achieved by outcome, although for some of the Communication, Language and Literacy strands and Mathematical Development strands, extension activities are suggested for older or more confident learners.

### Suggested teaching sequence for each unit

Each week has been organised into a suggested teaching sequence. However, each activity in an area of learning links to other activities and there will be overlap as groups engage with the tasks.

### The Core Curriculum: Literacy and Mathematics

Every school will have its own programmes for literacy and mathematics and it is not intended that the activities in the units in this book should replace these. Rather, the activities suggested aim to support any programme, to help to consolidate the learning and to demonstrate how the learning can be used in practical situations.

## The importance of role play

'Children try out their most recent learning, skills and competences when they play. They seem to celebrate what they know.'

*Tina Bruce (2001) Learning Through Play: Babies, Toddlers and the Foundation Years. London: Hodder & Stoughton.*

Early Years practitioners are aware of the importance of play as a vehicle for learning. When this play is carefully structured and managed then the learning opportunities are greatly increased. Adult participation can be the catalyst for children's imaginations and creativity.

Six weeks allows for a role play area to be created, developed and expanded and is the optimum time for inspiring children and holding their interest. It is important not to be too prescriptive in the role play area. Teachers should allow for children's ideas and interests to evolve and allow time for the children to explore and absorb information. Sometimes, the children will take the topic off at a tangent or go into much greater depth than expected or even imagined.

### Organising the classroom

The role play area could be created by partitioning off a corner of the classroom with ceiling drapes, an old-style clothes-horse, chairs, boxes, large-scale construction blocks (for example, 'Quadro') or even an open-fronted beach tent/shelter. Alternatively, the whole classroom could be dedicated to the role play theme.

### Involving parents and carers

Encourage the children to talk about the topic and what they are learning with their parents or carers at home. With adult help and supervision, they can explore the internet and search for pictures in magazines and books. This enriches the learning taking place in the classroom.

### Outside activities

The outdoor classroom should be an extension of the indoor classroom and it should support and enhance the activities offered inside. Boys, in particular, often feel less restricted in outdoor play. They may use language more purposefully and may even engage more willingly in reading and writing activities. In the

# Introduction

outdoor area things can be done on a much bigger, bolder and noisier scale and this may connect with boys' preferred learning styles.

Observation in Salford schools and settings noted that boys access books much more readily when there is a book area outdoors.

## Resources

Role play areas can be more convincing reconstructions when they are stocked with authentic items. Car boot sales, jumble sales and charity shops are good sources of artefacts. It is a good idea to inform parents and carers of topics well in advance so they can be looking out for objects and materials that will enhance the role play area.

## Reading

Every week there should be a range of opportunities for children to participate in reading experiences. These should include:

*Shared reading*

The practitioner should read aloud to the children from Big Books, modelling the reading process; for example, demonstrating that print is read from left to right. Shared reading also enables the practitioner to draw attention to high frequency words, the spelling patterns of different words and punctuation. Where appropriate, the practitioner should cover words and ask the children to guess which word would make sense in the context. This could also link with phonic work where the children could predict the word based on seeing the initial phoneme. Multiple readings of the same text enable them to become familiar with story language and tune in to the way written language is organised into sentences.

*Independent reading*

As children become more confident with the written word they should be encouraged to recognise high frequency words. Practitioners should draw attention to these words during shared reading and shared writing. Children should have the opportunity to read these words in context and to play word matching and word recognition games. Encourage the children to use their ability to hear the sounds at various points in words and to use their knowledge of those phonemes to decode simple words.

## Writing

*Shared writing*

Writing opportunities should include teacher demonstration, teacher scribing, copy writing and independent writing. (Suggestions for incorporating shared writing are given each week.)

*Emergent writing*

The role play area should provide ample opportunities for children to write purposefully, linking their writing with the task in hand. These meaningful writing opportunities help children to understand more about the writing process and to seek to communicate in writing. Children's emergent writing should occur alongside their increasing awareness of the 'correct' form of spellings. In the example below, the child is beginning to have an understanding of letter shapes as well as the need to write from left to right.

## Assessment

When children are actively engaged in the role play area this offers ample opportunities for practitioners to undertake observational assessments. By participating in the role play area the practitioner can take time to talk in role to the children about their work and assess their performance. The assessment grid on page 38 enables practitioners to record progress through the appropriate Stepping Stone or Early Learning Goal.

## DfES publications

The following publications will be useful:

*Progression in Phonics* (DfES 0178/2000)
*Developing Early Writing* (DfES 0055/2001)
*Playing with Sounds* (DfES 0280/2004)

## 'Fairy tales' planning chart

| Fairy tales | Role play area | Personal, Social and Emotional Development | Communication, Language and Literacy | Knowledge and Understanding of the World | Mathematical Development | Creative Development | Physical Development |
|---|---|---|---|---|---|---|---|
| Week 1 | Make the dwarfs' cottage and queen's castle | *Have developing awareness of their needs … be sensitive to the views of others* Talk about love and jealousy | *Use a pencil and form most letters correctly* Write names of dwarfs and make labels | *Identify features in the natural world* Talk about forests Look at different trees Walk in wood or country park | *Find one more or one less from 1 to 10* Look at groups of seven Addition and subtraction Use combination of coins to buy new hair band | *Explore colours and textures in two or three dimensions* Create cottage, window, queen's castle and mirror | *Move with confidence, imagination and in safety* Sing songs Play 'Follow my leader' |
| Week 2 | Make equipment for the cottage | *Consider consequences of their words and actions* Talk about feeling afraid, friendship and obedience | *Retell narrative in correct sequential order* Watch video of Snow White and the Seven Dwarfs Retell events | *Look closely at similarities and patterns of change* What happens to apples when they are cooked in different ways? | *Recreate simple patterns* Make patterns of seven Sort and count objects | *Use imagination in … role play* Make a cooker Make tools for dwarfs Make meal for dwarfs | *Travel around, under, over and through equipment* Build a castle and cottage with construction kits Move outside through the 'woods' |
| Week 3 | Make Jack's cottage | *Continue to be excited and motivated to learn* Circle time – what was it like to be poor a long time ago and what is it like today? | *Sustain attentive listening* Read Jack and the Beanstalk to class Letter sounds Lists | *Find out about features of living things* Look at and grow beans Cook and taste beans | *Use language – 'greater' and 'smaller'* Measure and count | *Use imagination in art and design* Make inside of Jack's house, the beanstalk and the giant | *Move with confidence, imagination and in safety* Partners copy each other's movements |
| Week 4 | Make the harp, the hen, the golden eggs and the bag of coins | *Understand what is right and what is wrong* Talk about stealing and excitement | *Listen with enjoyment and respond to stories* Read rhyming story of Jack and the Beanstalk Make cupboard book | *Investigate objects and materials by using senses* Look at harp and listen to harp music | *Use language of 'more' and 'less'* Count more and less Estimate and check by counting size of footprints | *Recognise and explore how sounds can be changed* Make a harp, hen and golden eggs Listen to and change musical sounds | *Handle objects with increasing control* Play the beans game Play instruments |
| Week 5 | Make Cinderella's fire and house and the prince's palace | *Work as part of a group, taking turns and sharing fairly* Talk about fairness and taking turns | *Respond to what they have heard with relevant comments and questions* Watch video of Cinderella Write invitations to the ball | *Find out about past and present events* Talk about ways of telling the time in the past and present Dances now and then | *Say and use number names* Tell the time Subtraction | *Explore colour, shape and texture in two or three dimensions* Create background and interior of palace | *Use a range of small and large equipment* Learn the waltz Play with the parachute |
| Week 6 | Have a banquet | *Form good relations with adults and peers* Talk about going to a party Look at manners | *Enjoy listening to spoken and written language and turn to it in role play* Share books about many traditional tales Write poem | *Ask questions about why things happen* Make food for banquet and discuss what happens during cooking | *Use language of 'smaller' to compare sizes* Look at size Positional language Counting | *Express and communicate ideas through design and songs* Lay table for a banquet Junk models | *Move with confidence, imagination and control* Dance to different music Play party games Eat the banquet |

# Fairy tales

During this six-week unit, the children will explore three traditional fairy tales – Snow White and the Seven Dwarfs, Jack and the Beanstalk and Cinderella. They will learn about imaginary castles and palaces, lands that exist out of time, magic that can solve problems and the form of traditional tales. They will discuss the importance of telling the truth, obedience, fairness and good manners.

In preparation for the unit, collect a range of costumes and props – dresses (bridesmaid, princess); adult-size coloured T-shirts; dwarfs' hats (long cones of fabric or long ski hats); belts or sashes of fabric; cloaks; a waistcoat and hat for the huntsman in Snow White; wellington boots.

At the end of the unit the children will have

- made the inside of the dwarfs' cottage
- decorated a magic mirror
- built a beanstalk from floor to ceiling
- made a pumpkin, mice, coach and clock
- made the inside of a fairy castle with chandelier and candelabra.
- drawn a life-size castle
- made a cooker, tools and meals for the dwarfs
- created a giant, harp, hen and golden eggs
- had a banquet with food and dance

## WEEK 1

### Starting the role play area

During this week the children will be introduced to the story of Snow White and the Seven Dwarfs. The role play area will become the dwarfs' cottage in the forest. They will make a **window frame scene** for the wall of the cottage and add **patterns in sevens** to the wallpaper. The **queen's castle** will be created at the entrance to the cottage. The children will take on the roles of characters in the story to explore emotions and friendship, communication and drama.

# Cottage and castle

## Resources

**Photocopiable:**

The dwarf outline and equipment (page 31)

**Fiction books:**

*A First Book of Fairy Tales* retold by Mary Hoffman, Dorling Kindersley (0 751328 07 3)
*First Fairy Tales* retold by Margaret Mayo, Orchard Books (1 843624 00 1)

**Non-fiction books:**

*I Feel Jealous* by Brian Moses, Hodder Wayland (0 750214 05 8)
*Forest*, 'Eye Wonder' series, Dorling Kindersley (1 405300 91 4)
*The Secret Life of Trees* by Chiara Chevallier, Dorling Kindersley (0 751362 11 5)
*Woodlands* by R and L Spilsbury, 'Wild Britain' series, Heinemann Library (0 431039 04 6)

**Poetry:**

*Mud Between the Toes* by Wendy Cooling, Franklin Watts (0 749650 07 9) – a collection of poems on 'feelings'

**Materials:**

- Dwarfs' costumes (very simple and inexpensive dwarfs' outfits can be created from adult-size T-shirts, belted or tied at the middle with an old scarf or sash of fabric; hats can be made by sewing two long triangles of fabric to make a cone shape – measure the circumference of a child's head first the edge can be rolled up to fit others)
- Table and seven small chairs
- Seven cups, knives, forks, spoons and plates
- Large safety mirror such as a floor-standing, full length, adjustable mirror available from most educational catalogues
- Dressing-up box, trolley or hooks and coat hangers
- Seven small 'blankets' or pieces of fabric
- Posters of forests/woods and trees
- Whiteboards
- Coins – 1p, 2p and 5p
- Printing pad and paint (to make a printing pad, take a shallow tray, such as a plastic meat tray, and place a layer of thin foam sponge on the bottom; mix up a fairly thick paint and soak into the sponge)
- Shades of green tissue paper
- Beads and so on, for crowns

**ICT:**

*Snow White and the Seven Dwarfs*, video or DVD, Disney

## Personal, Social and Emotional Development

*Have a developing awareness of their needs, views and feelings and be sensitive to the needs, views and feelings of others.*

### Circle time

- Ask the children: Who loves you? Give each child the opportunity to contribute. Ask: Who do you love? Talk about our families and how we are loved by them. Our mums /dads/ carers care for us.
- Ask the children if they know what it means if we say someone is vain. Explain the meaning of vanity and being vain. We like to look our best and be proud of ourselves, but we should see the good in others too. Ask: Is it good or bad to be vain?
- Tell the children that they will be hearing a story about a little girl called Snow White who lived in a castle with the queen, her stepmother. Explain what a stepmother is. Tell them that this story is a fairy tale about imaginary people. Stepmothers are not really unkind. The story is quite sad at the beginning but has a very happy ending. Ask the children if they know any other stories like that.
- Talk about jealousy. Ask the children if they have ever felt jealous. Tell them that the queen was a jealous person and that it did not make her feel happy.

## Communication, Language and Literacy

*Use a pencil and hold it effectively to form recognisable letters, most of which are correctly formed.*

### Listening

- Read a version of the story 'Snow White and the Seven Dwarfs' (see Resources). Encourage the children to talk about the story. Ask: Did you like the story? Which part did you like best? Was it a happy or a sad story? Do you think it was a true story about real people? Talk again about fairy tales. They are make-believe.

# Cottage and castle

- Show short excerpts from the Disney film. Explain that this version gave the dwarfs names: Dopey, Sleepy, Happy, Grumpy, Sneezy, Doc and Bashful. Those names described the characters the film portrayed. Explain the meaning of 'bashful', 'dopey' and 'grumpy'. Who were the other characters in the story – prince, huntsman, queen?
- Reread the story and encourage the children to join in with the rhyme, 'Mirror, mirror, on the wall'.

### Writing: teacher demonstration

- Make labels on folded card with the name of each dwarf. Talk about letter formation as you write. Ask the children to copy the capital letter formation in the air, pointing with the index finger of their writing hand. When they have done this several times, ask them to write the letter on their whiteboards while you write the rest of the name. Use these labels to place on chairs or at the top of each 'bed'.
- Make laminated name cards for each dwarf, the queen, the prince and Snow White. Punch a hole in each and thread ribbon to make pendants. Children should wear the appropriate pendant when entering the role play area.

- 'Dwarfs' can match their names with the folded cards (see above) to sit in 'their' chair or sleep in 'their' bed.

### Extension

- Ask some children to make labels for the role play area: 'window', 'Seven Dwarfs' Cottage', 'chair', 'castle' and 'mirror'. Help them to form the letters large enough for the rest of the class to read.

### Writing: teacher scribing

- Look at pictures of dwarfs in the story and talk about them. Ask the children to think of words to describe them. Scribe these on a whiteboard.
- Make copies of the picture of a dwarf and his equipment (page 31) and glue them onto thicker card. Cut these out to make templates for the children. Give each child a template of a dwarf and an A4 sheet of card. Ask them to draw round the template and cut out their dwarf. They should then write the name of the dwarf. (Save the pictures of the equipment for Mathematical Development.)

## Creative Development

 *Explore colours, textures, shapes, form and space in two or three dimensions.*

### Creating the cottage

- You will need enough backing paper in a light, bright colour – for example, yellow or pale blue – to line the walls of the role play area. On this background, print simple wallpaper patterns. You will need a printing pad and paint (see Resources) and some objects for printing with, such as Unifix cubes, corks or cotton reels. Do the prints in blocks of seven, randomly over the background.
- Create a window looking out into the forest. Ask the children where they would like their window to be in the cottage. Decide with them the size and shape it will be – round, square or rectangular. Cut the window out of white paper or card (one metre square or larger). Ask a child to draw the horizon where the sky and ground will meet. (Explain the meaning of 'horizon' first and try to show them through a window or by pictures.) Using a sponge and shades of blue paint, print the sky. Again using a sponge, but with shades of green and brown, print the ground. Ask the children to paint trees and cut them out. Have available scraps of different shades of green tissue paper. Show the children how to tear leaves and stick them onto their trees. Glue the trees onto the ground to create a forest. Use strips of yellow or white border paper to make the window frame. Glue or staple the window onto the wall. Staple fabric curtains to either side. (This window will be replaced by another in week 3, so try to fix it so that it can be removed easily.)

Starting with role play – Fairy tales  9

# Cottage and castle

- Put a table and seven small chairs in the cottage. Put seven pieces of fabric or blankets in the cottage to be used as dwarfs' beds.

## Creating the castle

- Show the children pictures of fairy tale castles and ask them to design their own. Make these pictures into a book of castles. Make the covers of the book a simple castle shape. Choose one of the designs and ask the 'designer' to draw a large version on a long sheet of card or paper (this could reach from floor to ceiling). Paint the castle grey. Print stone blocks in shades of grey on top. Display at the side of the entrance to the cottage.

## The mirror

- Make a frame for the mirror (see Resources). Measure round the edge, cut strips of card long enough to form the frame. Cut a wavy line along one side to form the outside edge of the frame. Paint the card with PVA glue. Press swirls of wool and/or string into the glue to make an ornate pattern. When completely dry, paint all over with gold paint. Fix around the frame of the mirror with sticky tack. Place the mirror in front of the castle.

## Crowns

- Make a crown for the queen and the prince by decorating strips of gold or silver card with cotton wool, coloured beads, sequins and jewel shapes cut from coloured foil. Staple into a headband.

### Mathematical Development

 *Find one more or one less than a number from 1 to 10.*

## Counting

- In the cottage, look at the groups of seven you can see on the walls. Count to check as some may have been covered up.
- Ask the children to set the table for the seven dwarfs. They will need seven cups, plates, knives, forks and spoons. Ask the children to count the sevens as they put out the various items.
- Snow White is joining the dwarfs for dinner. How many more of each item will you need to put on the table? Will there be enough chairs for everyone?

## Addition and subtraction games

- You will need seven copies of the dwarf and his equipment (page 31) pasted onto cards. Laminate them if possible. Spread out face up the seven dwarf cards and the seven hat cards. Ask the children the following: Can you give each dwarf a hat? How many dwarfs and how many hats are there? If we take one hat away, will there be enough hats for each dwarf? Challenge the children to try it. Say: Here are four hats. How many dwarfs will not get one to wear? Do the same with the cards of the dwarfs' equipment. Ask: Five dwarfs have a spade to take to do their work. How many more do we need so that they all have one?

### Extension

- Count in sevens on a number square. Tell the children to count in sevens and colour, ring or place a counter on each multiple of seven. Ask: Can you see the diagonal pattern? What would happen if you started counting sevens from another number?

## Money

- You will need 1p, 2p and 5p coins. NB: children will need plenty of input and practical activities so that they have a thorough knowledge of the value of each coin before they attempt the following task.

# Cottage and castle

- Explain that one of the dwarfs is going to the market to buy Snow White a new hair band. It costs 7p. He has a purse full of 1p, 2p and 5p coins. How many different ways can he pay for the hair band? For example; 5p, 1p and 1p, or 2p, 2p, 1p, 1p and 1p.

## Knowledge and Understanding of the World

 *Observe, find out about and identify features in ... the natural world.*

### Forests

- Explain that the dwarfs lived in a little cottage in the forest. Ask the children to tell you what they know about forests. Ask: Who or what else might live in a forest? What is the difference between a wood and a forest? Why do you think there are not as many forests in the world as there used to be?
- If possible, take the children for a walk in a wood or a local country park. Ask: What can you see? How do you know that animals live here? How do you think Snow White must have felt when she was left all alone in the forest? If a visit is not possible, look at the trees in the school grounds and show posters of forests and woods.
- Talk about the different trees in the woods. Try to identify and name some of them. Snow White had hair as black as ebony. Explain that ebony is a very hard, dark wood not found growing in the UK.

## Physical Development

 *Move with confidence, imagination and in safety.*

### Singing

- Teach the children the song:
  Heigh-ho Heigh-ho
  It's off to work we go
  We keep on singing all day long
  Heigh-ho Heigh-ho
  Heigh-ho Heigh-ho
  Heigh-ho Heigh-ho

Repeat with the line 'It's home from work we go'. (Some children may be able to accompany the others by whistling!) Remind the children that the dwarfs walked to work, singing as they went. For a full version of the song see www.stlyrics.com.

### Follow my leader

- Put the children into groups of seven, as far as possible. Ask one to be the leader and to choose a way of moving – walking, big steps, small steps, skipping, marching and so on. Tell the others to follow in the same way, weaving in and out of the spaces and paths of other groups.
- When the dwarfs get to work, they dig and sieve the earth, looking for gold. Mime these actions, as a group, following the leader's movements. Change leaders and repeat.

*Starting with role play – Fairy tales*

# Fairy tales

## WEEK 2

### The role play area

During this week the children will, through role play in the dwarfs' cottage, explore emotions such as feeling frightened and being sorry. They will become aware of the importance of doing as they are told.

They will make a **cooker** and **miners' tools** which will be displayed on the wall. They will search for **gold nuggets** and make **pretend meals** for the dwarfs. They will also make **wooden spoon puppets** to use to act out the story.

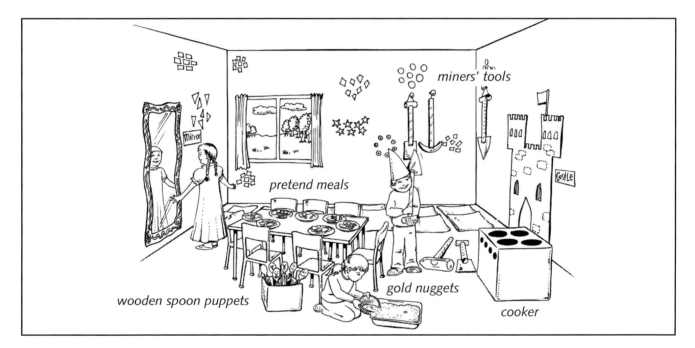

### Resources

Photocopiables:

The dwarfs' equipment (page 31)
Poems and rhymes 1 (page 32)
Puppets and beanstalk (page 34)

Fiction book:

*Into the Castle* by June Crebbin, Walker Books (0 744552 35 4)

Non-fiction book:

*I Feel Frightened* by Brian Moses, Hodder Wayland (0 750214 04 X)

Music and songs:

*Big Steps, Little Steps* (CD and song books) by Mary E Mauder, Kindescope (www.kindescope.com)
'Who's afraid?', 'When I feel sad' and 'Friends' from *The Handy Band* by Sue Nicholls, A & C Black (0 713668 97 0)

ICT:

*Snow White and the Seven Dwarfs*, Video or DVD, Disney

Materials:

- Box
- Collection of kitchen equipment
- Toy tools such as spades, forks and rakes
- Face paints (baby lotion and small amount of ready-mix paint)
- Cotton buds
- Facial tissues
- Wooden spoons
- Apples, brown and white sugar, raisins, ready-made pastry
- Paper plates
- Sand tray

# Cottage equipment

## Personal, Social and Emotional Development

 *Consider the consequences of their words and actions for themselves and others.*

### Circle time

- Talk about feeling afraid. Ask: How do you think Snow White felt when she was left all alone in the forest? Have you ever felt afraid?
- Sing 'Who's afraid?' from *The Handy Band* (see Resources). Sing 'When I feel sad' (tune Aiken Drum), also from *The Handy Band*.

### Friendship

- Talk about how Snow White found some friends, the dwarfs. They looked after her. Ask: Who are your friends? Why do you like them?
- Chant 'Friends' from *The Handy Band* (see Resources).
- Read and discuss the poem 'I'd be a good friend' (see page 33).

### Keeping safe

- The dwarfs told Snow White not to open the door to strangers. They wanted to keep her safe. Ask: Did she do as she was told? What happened? Parents and carers often tell us to do or not do things. Discuss why it is important for children to do as they are told.
- We are told not to talk to strangers but there are some people who we can talk to if, for example, we are lost in a shop or the street. Ask the children who they could ask for help.

## Creative Development

 *Use their imagination in role play.*

### Making a cooker

- Paint a box white and add circles of black card to represent the hob and control knobs. (The children could draw round circle templates and cut them out.) Place the cooker against a wall in the cottage.
- Make a collection of kitchen equipment such as a saucepan, frying pan, ladle, colander and kettle.

### Painting and design

- Give the children pieces of paper, about A3 size, and ask them to choose one of the kitchen items to draw, cut out and paint. Display these on the 'kitchen wall' of the cottage above the cooker.
- Explain that the dwarfs need to have different tools for their work and that they keep them neatly hanging on a wall in their cottage. Provide cardboard tubes, foil wrap and junk modelling resources. Ask the children to work in pairs to make model tools. They could make a spade, fork, rake, pickaxe or sieve. Fix these in neat rows to the other wall of the cottage. Place a few toy tools on the floor for the 'dwarfs' to carry and use in their imaginative role play.
- Tell the children that Snow White and the prince are to be married. Ask them to design a wedding dress for Snow White or a wedding outfit for the prince.

### Face painting

- Have available at the entrance to the cottage a small range of face paints and cotton buds. As the children enter the role play area, they should establish the roles they will take on. An adult should be on hand to help them here. Those taking on the role of a dwarf or Snow White should paint red circles on their cheeks. The 'queen' should paint a disguise. Encourage the children to do their own face painting and to use the mirror. (To make face paints, see Resources.)
- Remind the children that they must throw away used cotton buds and should remove face paint

# Cottage equipment

when they have finished playing. (Face paint can be easily removed with tissues and baby lotion.) NB: it would be useful to have a bin next to the mirror.

### Making a meal for the dwarfs and Snow White

❑ You will need paper plates and collage materials (such as yellow wool for spaghetti, matchsticks for chips, tissue paper to create peas, large beads for potatoes and card for pizza). Discuss possible meal ideas and then ask the children to create a meal and glue it onto a plate. Place the plates in the cottage for the children to use in their role play.

### Making wooden spoon puppets

❑ See page 34 for instructions. Store the puppets in the cottage for story telling and role play.

### Outdoor play

❑ On a dry day, take the mirror, table and seven chairs outside and encourage imaginative play in a larger space.

## Mathematical Development

 *Talk about, recognise and recreate simple patterns.*

### Counting

❑ Have prepared some gold nuggets – these could be wooden beads painted with gold paint or gold foil scrunched into balls. Hide the gold nuggets in the sand tray. Provide scoops and sieves. Ask the children to pretend that they are dwarfs searching for gold and to count how many nuggets they have found.

❑ As above, but use a one-minute sand timer. Challenge the children to find as many nuggets as possible in one minute.

❑ Look at the dots on a dice. Tell the children to count the dots on each side. Ask the children if they could make a count of seven if they rolled another dice. Challenge them to try it. Which numbers add up to seven? Write the numbers on a whiteboard. Challenge the children to see how many sevens they can roll in one minute.

### Patterns

❑ Make patterns of seven with the nuggets. Change the patterns. Ask: Are there still seven nuggets in your pattern?

### Sorting

❑ Have available a selection of apples - some green, some red, some large and some small. Ask the children to sort them by size and colour.

### Pairs

❑ Make several copies of the illustration of a dwarf's hat on page 31 (you need an even number of cards, say eight). Colour the cards in different colours – there should be two cards of each colour. Spread the cards face down on the table in the cottage. Ask the children to turn over two cards to find pairs.

**Extension**

❑ When the children have formed all the pairs, ask them to count in twos. How many cards are there?

## Communication, Language and Literacy

 *Retell narrative in the correct sequence, drawing on language patterns of stories.*

### Sequencing the story

❑ Show short excerpts from the Disney version of Snow White and the Seven Dwarfs and reread some parts of the story to remind the children of the

# Cottage equipment

events. Help them to recall the main events in sequence. Ask them to tell you what happened at the beginning of the story, what happened next and how the story ended.

**Extension**

❑ Draw a line about half way down a piece of A3 paper. Allocate different episodes of the story to different children. They draw their part of the story above the line. Help them to write a sentence underneath. Look at the pictures and sentences and discuss the sequence with the children. Ask them to help you display the pictures in the correct order in the classroom or make them into a class book.

## Following directions

❑ You will need a gold nugget (a chocolate coin would be ideal). Tell the class to sit together in a group. Ask one child to leave the room and then another child to hide the nugget in the room. Ask the first child to return to the classroom and search for the gold. Tell the class to help the search by calling out 'warm', 'warmer', 'hot', 'very hot', 'cold', 'colder', 'freezing'. 'Very hot' is very close to the gold!

## Retelling the story

❑ Tell the story of Snow White with puppets (see Creative Development). Demonstrate using the puppets while you tell the story and then let the children have a go in the role play area.

## Knowledge and Understanding of the World

 *Look closely at similarities, differences, patterns and change.*

## Apples

❑ Remind the children that the queen gave Snow White an apple to eat. That apple was not very nice! Ask: Do you like apples? Where do apples come from?

❑ The dwarfs liked apples too. They liked raw apples, stewed apples, baked apples and apple sauce with their roast pork. Explain to the children that they are going to cook some apples for the dwarfs.

❑ In groups, cook apples in different ways – for example, one group could prepare cooking apples and stew them; another could prepare cooking apples to bake either in the oven or in a microwave (core, score round the middle and fill the centre with raisins and brown sugar); another could make an apple pie (use ready-made pastry).

❑ Observe and talk about the changes to the apples when cooked.

❑ Take the children into the cottage, in groups of seven, if possible. Each child should take on the role of a dwarf (wear a hat!), sit at the table and taste the cooked apples. Ask: Which did you like the best? Was the apple still crunchy?

## Physical Development

 *Travel around, under, over and through balancing equipment.*

## Building

❑ Challenge the children to build a castle with a construction kit with large building blocks and then a cottage with small bricks, such as Lego.

## Movement

❑ Sing and move to the *Big Steps, Little Steps* CD (see Resources).

## Outside

❑ Place two or three benches in the playground and explain that these are fallen trees. Tell the children to pretend that they are the dwarfs weaving in and out of the trees as they go to work. They could walk along the fallen trees, step over them or walk around them. Encourage them to move in different ways – running with little steps/big steps, walking and turning, and striding high and low.

❑ Ask the girls to stand in spaces, arms outstretched as trees in the forest. Tell the boys to pretend to be the dwarfs weaving in and out of the trees, ducking under the branches. Change over so that the boys are the trees and the girls the dwarfs. Vary the movements as practised.

# Fairy tales

## WEEK 3

### The role play area

During this week the children will be introduced to the story of Jack and the Beanstalk. The dwarfs' cottage will become Jack's cottage. They will make a **new window scene**, a **beanstalk** that reaches up to the ceiling and the **giant**. The children will consider what it might be like to be very poor.

### Resources

Photocopiables:

Poems and rhymes 1 (page 32)
The beanstalk (page 34)

Fiction books:

*Jack and the Beanstalk* by Margaret Mayo, First Fairy Tales series, Orchard Books (1 841211 46 X)
*Jasper's Beanstalk* by Nick Butterworth and Mick Inkpen, Hodder Wayland (0 340586 34 6)

Non-fiction books:

*My Bean Diary* by Monica Hughes, 'Discovery World Big Books' series, Heinemann (0 435097 92 X)
*Life Cycle of a Broad Bean* by Angela Royston, Heinemann Library (0 431083 63 0)

Music and songs:

*Michael Finnigin, Tap Your Chinigin* by Sue Nicholls, A & C Black (0 713647 16 7)

Materials:

- Ring, fixed to the ceiling or high on a wall
- Shawls
- Old clothes such as waistcoats, men's shirts, skirts or dresses
- Adult trousers
- Belts or cord
- Plaster of Paris
- Net curtain rings (eyes)
- Dowel, approximately 1cm diameter, cut into approximately 35cm lengths
- Green tissue paper
- Runner beans to grow
- Clear plastic container
- Blotting paper
- A piece of black fabric for the 'cow'
- Adult-size wellington boots (two pairs – one to make a giant and one for the 'giant' to wear in the role play area)
- Coin bags (from a bank)
- Tape recorder
- Digital camera

**16 Starting** with role play – Fairy tales

# Jack's cottage

## Communication, Language and Literacy

*Sustain attentive listening, responding to what they have heard with relevant comments.*

### Listening

- Read a version of the story Jack and the Beanstalk (see Resources).
- Talk about the story and why Jack 'stole' the giant's treasures. (In some versions, the giant had stolen from Jack's father years ago, so Jack thought the treasure was rightly his and his mother's.) Tell the children that there are many versions of fairy tales because parents have told them to their children for generations and they have been changed slightly over the years.
- Explain that they are going to pretend to be a mum or a dad and tell the story of Jack and the Beanstalk to their children. Ask a confident child to tell the story to the class. Record his retelling on a tape recorder. Ask another adult to take individual children into the role play area to record their retellings. The adult can act as the child by asking questions to prompt (such as: What happened next?). Play back some of these tapes. Ask: Was the story always the same or were there different versions?

### Writing lists

- Place writing materials and an exercise book in the cottage for Jack and his mother to write wish lists. Write 'I wish I could have' at the top of the pages. Encourage the children to write or draw their wish.

### Letter sounds

- Explain to the children that you are going to write some labels for the cottage and you want them to help you. Ask the children to tell you the initial sound in each of the following – cow, beanstalk, beans, Jack, giant, cottage, castle, egg, harp and gold. Write the letters and ask them to make the shape of the letter in the air using their index finger. Write the full labels for the class and make a second set for matching.

### Extension

- Ask the children to help you spell some of the labels. Ask them to tell you how many phonemes there are in each word – for example, Jack = J–a–ck = 3; gold = g–o–l–d = 4. Help them to write some of the labels.

## Personal, Social and Emotional Development

*Continue to be interested, excited and motivated to learn.*

### Circle time

- Remind the children about how poor Jack and his mother were. One day his mother told him that they had nothing left but the cottage and a cow. Ask the children to imagine what it must be like to be so poor. Imagine not having enough to eat. Ask: What things would you really miss if you were poor? How do you think Jack and his mother felt when they realised they would have to sell their faithful cow?
- Ask each child to tell you about one thing that they have that they like. Talk about the many people in the world who are poor and starving or have no proper home to live in.
- Encourage the children to talk about being poor when they are playing in the cottage as Jack, his friends or his mother. Encourage them to talk to the 'cow' – for example, saying how sorry they are to have to sell her.

## Creative Development

*Sing simple songs from memory. Use imagination in art and design.*

### Music and songs

- Sing 'Run, Jack, run' (see page 32) and encourage the children to learn it by heart.
- Sing and play 'Leaping and stepping' from *Michael Finnigin, Tap Your Chinigin* (see Resources).

Starting with role play – Fairy tales  17

# Jack's cottage

### Making the inside of Jack's house

- Remove from the cottage five of the chairs, the window and curtains, the 'beds', and the queen's, prince's and dwarfs' costumes. Find a picture of a cow, put it in a photo frame and display on the cottage wall.

### Creating the window: clouds

- Decide with the children the shape and size the window will be. Make it slightly larger than for the dwarfs' cottage to cover up marks on the background. Either use light blue paper or paint a wash of blue over white paper to create the sky. Ask the children to draw cloud shapes on white card and cut them out. Have ready cut small circles of white tissue paper and/or white gummed paper. Glue the circles all over the clouds with glue sticks. Stick the clouds onto the blue sky at the top. Bend some of the clouds to give depth.

### Creating the window: beanstalk

- Take two strips of green crepe paper. Twist each one; then twist the two strips together and glue them onto the background, starting at the bottom of the paper and hiding the top under a cloud. Have ready cut leaf shapes in various shades of green tissue. Glue just the base of the leaves and stick onto the stalk. Staple the window to the background of the cottage and make a frame with border paper. Staple dull, worn or torn fabric at either side for the curtains.

### Making the beanstalk

- Create a 'growing' beanstalk for the classroom (see page 34).
- Help the children to make individual beanstalks (see page 34).

### Create the giant

- You will need a pair of old adult-size wellington boots, a pair of old trousers and newspaper. Stretch an elastic band around the bottom of each trouser leg. Push the legs into the boots and stuff the legs with newspaper. Staple or sew the waist to seal. Make sure that the boots won't fall off! (You may have to use a liberal amount of double-sided sticky tape inside the top of each boot to secure them.) Staple the giant as close to the ceiling as possible, as if he is climbing down the beanstalk. Take some white fabric and create clouds to hide the top of the trousers.

> ## Mathematical Development
>  Use language such as 'greater' and 'smaller' to compare sizes.

### Large and small

- Encourage the children to use the language of size – for example, a giant is huge. Ask: What else is huge? What other words describe very big things? (Enormous, gigantic, vast, massive.) Can you think of some things that are very small? What other words describe very small things? (Minute, tiny.)

### Measuring

- Measure and cut string for mini beanstalks (see Creative Development).

### Counting

- Give out real packets of beans for the children to count. Ask: Do all the bags have the same number of beans inside? Why do you think they may have different numbers inside?

# Jack's cottage

- Collect coin bags (from the bank!) Stick a label on each bag, with a number from 1 to 10. Provide a tray of real beans. Ask the children to put the correct number of beans into each bag and then to check each other's bags.

**Extension**

- Put ten beans in a tray. Sit two children in front of the tray. Ask: If you are going to share these beans between you, will you both have the same number of beans? Encourage the children to try it. Vary the number of beans in the tray and the number of children, according to ability.

## Knowledge and Understanding of the World

 *Find out about, and identify, some features of living things.*

### Beans

- Share either a fiction or a non-fiction book about beans with the class (see Resources).
- Show the children some runner beans and explain that these are the sort of beans that Jack was given in exchange for the cow. Tell the children that they are going to grow these beans to see who will have the tallest beanstalk.
- Give groups of children a clear plastic container and some kitchen paper. Show them how to line the container with the kitchen paper and place a bean approximately halfway down between the paper and the container. Explain that it is each group's responsibility to water the beans but they should be careful not to overwater.

- When the beans have grown to about 15–20cm in height, plant them in the ground or a pot and support them with canes and twine. If possible, take photographs of the beans and display these in the classroom. (If they are in a pot, the children can take them home to look after during the holidays.)

### Cooking beans

- If possible, show the children some runner beans in their pods. Explain that these are the beans that grow on the beanstalk. Tell the children that they are good for you and taste nice. Let the children touch and smell the beans.
- Show them how to prepare the beans for cooking. Top and tail, wash and slice them. Boil them in water so that they are cooked but still crunchy.
- Have a tasting session. Ask: What do the beans taste like? Do they smell any different now they are cooked? Did you like the taste?

## Physical Development

 *Move with confidence, imagination and in safety.*

### Movement

- Tell the children to work in pairs. Ask one child to be Jack and the other the giant. Jack creeps away from the giant. The giant follows, copying Jack. Jack begins to move faster and faster and the giant copies. Jack begins to slow down until he is creeping again and the giant copies. The aim is to keep the same distance between Jack and the giant, whatever the speed.

### Giant's treasure game

- Tell the children to sit in a circle, facing inwards. Ask one child to sit in the middle as the giant. Explain that the giant is asleep but he has his treasure right beside him. Place a bunch of keys or bells next to the giant. Blindfold the giant or ask him to close his eyes. Explain that someone, Jack, is going to try to steal the treasure and that everyone must stay very quiet and still. Point to a child in the circle. This child must stand up, as Jack, creep all the way round the outside of the circle, back through his space and up to steal the treasure. The giant has to listen very carefully. If he hears any movement, he points in the direction of the sound. If he points directly at Jack, Jack sits back in his place and another child has a go. If Jack manages to steal the treasure without being caught, he becomes the giant in the middle.

Starting *with role play – Fairy tales* 19

# Fairy tales

## WEEK 4

**The role play area**

During this week the children will make a **cupboard book**, the **harp**, the **hen**, **golden eggs** and the **bag of coins** to add to the role play area. They will explore elements of music in their imaginative role play.

### Resources

Photocopiable:

Poems and rhymes 2 (page 33)

Fiction books:

*Jack and the Beanstalk* by Nick Sharratt and Stephen Tucker, Macmillan (0 333962 18 4)
*Shhh!* by Sally Grindley, Hodder Wayland (0 340746 62 9)
*It's Not Fair* by Brian Moses, Hodder Wayland (0 750221 32 1)
*It Wasn't Me* by Brian Moses, Hodder Wayland (0 750221 35 6)

Music and song:

Harp music – for example, *Lullaby Harp* by Patricia Spero, New World (ASIN: B0000000BP)
'Jack and the beanstalk' from *Three Singing Pigs* by Kaye Umansky, A & C Black (0 713638 04 4)

Websites:

Google: images (type in 'harp')

Materials:

- Untuned percussion instruments
- Xylophone or set of chime bars
- Beans
- Paper eggs
- Gold paint
- Gold glitter
- Magazines (containing pictures of food and toys)

# Harps, hens and coins!

## Personal, Social and Emotional Development

 *Understand what is right, what is wrong and why.*

### Circle time

- Talk about how Jack went up the beanstalk to the giant's castle three times. Each time was an exciting adventure for him. Ask the children to discuss with a partner what they would do if they could do something really exciting. Ask: Where would you go? What would you do? Who would you take with you? Ask the children to take it in turns to share their ideas with the group.

- Remind the children that in the traditional story Jack stole the hen, the gold coins and the harp from the giant. Discuss with the class how it is wrong to take things that do not belong to you. Talk about how the person who has had something stolen feels. Ask: Why do you think people steal? What should you do if someone has taken something belonging to you? Talk about how easy it is to think that you have had something taken when really you have just lost it.

## Mathematical Development

 *Use language such as 'more' and 'less' to compare numbers.*

### Counting

- Put a number of coins in a bag – up to 20 if appropriate – and ask individual children to pretend they are the giant counting his coins. Ask: How many coins are in your bag?

- Play 'I don't want my beans!', a game for three or four players. Give each child 20 beans in a bowl or pot (you could use real beans, beads or counters). In the centre of the table place a pot or container. Tell the children to take it in turns to roll a dice and count the spots. They then count that number of beans from their bowl and put them in the pot in the centre. The winner is the child who gets rid of all their beans first.

- Draw on card and cut out footprints of different sizes – a child's, an adult's and a giant's. Laminate the cards if possible for durability. Have available a selection of small objects such as cotton reels, corks, small Lego bricks and Unifix blocks. Ask the children to cover the adult's footprint with, for example, Unifix blocks and to guess beforehand how many they will manage to fit on. Tell them to check by counting. Ask: Do you think you will need more or less blocks to cover the giant's footprint? Try it and count the blocks. Ask: Do you think you will need more or less cotton reels to cover the child's footprint?

- Play 'Race to the beanstalk', a game for two players. You will need two small bricks (one larger than the other), a coin with paper stuck on each side and a strip of A3 paper. Mark one side of the coin with 'Move 2' and the other with 'Move 1'. Draw the giant's face on a circle of paper and stick it onto the larger brick. Draw Jack's face on another circle and stick it onto the smaller brick. Draw a path down the sheet of A3 paper of 2 squares wide x 12 long. The squares should be large enough for the bricks to land on. At the beginning of the path draw a cottage and at the end of the path draw a beanstalk. Tell the children to take either 'Jack' or the 'giant' and place him on the first square of their path. They should take it in turns to toss the coin and move their playing piece accordingly. The winner is the first to reach the beanstalk at the end of the path.

- Read 'Giant's breakfast – a counting rhyme' (see page 33). Talk about the names of the numbers in the poem and write these as words for the children.

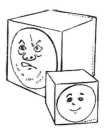

### Extension

- Ask the children to write the numbers as figures on their whiteboards as you say them.

*Starting* with role play – Fairy tales  21

# Harps, hens and coins!

## Communication, Language and Literacy

 *Listen with enjoyment and respond to stories, rhymes and poems.*

### Listening

- Read a story of Jack and the Beanstalk in rhyme, such as the one by Nick Sharratt and Stephen Tucker (see Resources).
- Ask the children if they enjoyed the story in rhyme. Ask: Were there any differences between this story and the one you heard last week? Do you prefer the story in rhyme? Copy one or two of the verses onto the board and ask them to identify the rhyming words. Encourage them to think of other words to rhyme with them.

### Making a cupboard book

- Remind the children that at the beginning of the story the cupboard was bare. Jack had no food to eat. At the end of the story Jack and his mother were very rich and could buy what they wanted.
- Tell the children that they are going to make a 'cupboard book'. They can put all the things that Jack and his mother can buy in the cupboard. Refer to the wish lists made in the role play area.
- Read out some of the things Jack and his mother had wished for. Ask the children for more ideas.
- Give each child a sheet of card, about A3 size, and show them how to fold the sides to the centre to make the cupboard doors. Label the front 'Jack's cupboard'. Colour two door handles. Draw shelves inside the cupboard, using a ruler. Ask the children to find pictures in catalogues and magazines to cut out and stick on the shelves.

### Extension

- Ask the children to write labels for each item. Show them how to use a ruler to draw an arrow to the different things on their shelves and to write the words at the end of the arrows.

## Knowledge and Understanding of the World

 *Investigate objects and materials by using their senses as appropriate.*

### The harp

- If possible, invite a harpist to demonstrate the instrument and style of music played on the harp.
- Show pictures of harps and play some harp music (see Resources). Explain how the sounds are made by plucking the different length strings.

### Experiment

- Demonstrate how sounds vary according to the different length and tautness of the strings, by stretching an elastic band from, for example, a door handle, and plucking it. Let the children experiment with this under adult supervision.
- Try the above with a thicker or thinner elastic band. Encourage the children to talk about their findings.

## Creative Development

 *Recognise and explore how sounds can be changed.*

### Making the harp

- Find a picture of a harp and ask a child to draw an outline on white A3 card, cut it out and paint it. Ask the child to paint the frame gold and to draw strings with a felt-tip pen and a ruler. When dry, repeat on the other side. Laminate the harp.

**Starting** with role play – Fairy tales

# Harps, hens and coins!

### Making the hen

❏ Find a picture of a hen and ask a child to draw an outline on A3 card. Cut it out. Ask the child to paint the hen in red and brown on both sides. Laminate the hen.

### Making the golden eggs

❏ You will need paper eggs (from hobby shops), gold paint, gold glitter and PVA glue. Ask the children to paint the eggs with gold paint. When it is dry, tell them to paint over the eggs with PVA glue and roll the eggs in gold glitter. They may need to touch up where the eggs have rested while drying.

### Bag of coins

❏ Fold a piece of fabric in two. Sew down the sides, leaving the top open. Fill with either chocolate or plastic coins. Twist an elastic band to seal it. Alternatively, use a small drawstring bag. Encourage the children to use their new props in their role play.

### Music

❏ Use voices as instruments to represent going up and down the beanstalk. (Ooh – up and down.) Tap the bars of a xylophone to go higher and lower. Tell the children that in musical terms this is called 'pitch'.

❏ Ask the children to sit in a circle. Place a drum, a tambourine, some bells and a maraca in the middle of the circle. Explain that the children must pass a golden egg round the circle as they sing (to the tune of Looby Loo):

Pass the egg around

Pass the egg around

Pass the egg around

_____?_____ can make a sound.

Whoever is holding the egg when the song finishes, goes to the middle. Say: _____?_____, can you play the drum quietly/loudly? Continue the song, passing the egg. Vary the instruments and dynamics.

❏ Ask three children to sit in the middle of the circle. Tell them that they are going to make a sequence of musical patterns. Give one (Jack) the bells, another (the giant) the drum and the third the xylophone or chime bars. Tell the children you are going to tell a story and they should listen very carefully and think where they might add in some music.

Say: Jack decided to climb the beanstalk to seek his fortune. He climbed and climbed right up to the top. He saw a castle and walked bravely to it. Then he tiptoed very quietly up to the giant to take the bag of coins. The giant was fast asleep. Jack picked up the bag of coins and began to tiptoe away. Suddenly, the giant woke up. He saw Jack. Oh no! He's going to chase him. Run, Jack, run! At last Jack reached the top of the beanstalk. He climbed down as quickly as he could. The giant stopped chasing and plodded slowly back to his castle. Phew! Jack was lucky that time!

## Physical Development

 *Handle objects with increasing control.*

### Experimenting with sounds and movement

❏ Using the musical instruments from Creative Development, ask the children to take turns to play an instrument quietly or loudly and make slow or quick patterns. The others move in ways suggested by the music.

❏ Play the beans game. The children stand in a circle. Tell each child what type of bean they are and explain the actions for each:
Broad beans: stand with feet and arms wide apart;
French beans: say 'Ooh la! la!' and wave hand;
String beans: make a tall, narrow shape;
Runner beans: run on the spot;
Kidney beans: make a curved shape;
Jelly beans: wobble;
Baked beans: drop to ground in small shape;
Frozen beans: freeze!

# Fairy tales

## WEEK 5

**The role play area**

During this week the children will be introduced to the story of Cinderella. The role play area will become a fairy tale castle. Cinderella's fireplace will be just outside the entrance to the castle. The children will make a **chandelier**, a **candelabra** and **headbands for horses**. They will draw and paint **pumpkins** and **mice**.

Week 5 involves a lot of artwork. If possible, invite parents to help the children by creating an art workshop: they do not need to be 'artists', just enthusiastic! They could also help you to set up the role play area as items are finished. Some might even become so involved that they want to join in with their children's role play!

### Resources

Photocopiables:

Poems and rhymes 2 (page 33)
The inside of the palace (pages 35–37)

Fiction books:

*Cinderella* by Margaret Mayo, 'First Fairy Tales' series, Orchard books (1 841211 50 8)
*Cinderella* by Nicola Baxter and Charles Perrault, Ladybird Favourite Tales (0 721416 92 6)
*Into the Castle* by June Crebbin, Walker Books (0 744552 35 4)
*Cinderella* by Nick Sharratt and Stephen Tucker, Macmillan (0 333965 33 7)

Music and songs:

*Bingo Lingo* by Helen MacGregor, A & C Black (0 713650 75 3)
*Three Tapping Teddies* by Kaye Umansky, A & C Black (0 713651 18 0)
*Tom Thumb's Musical Maths* by Helen MacGregor, A & C Black (0 713649 71 2)

Video/DVD:

*Cinderella* (Disney)

Materials:

- Fairy outfit or wings for the fairy godmother
- Dresses – bridesmaid if possible or just a selection of pretty or sparkling ones
- Apron and shawl for Cinderella
- Crown for the prince
- Shawls or lengths of fabric for the ugly sisters
- Hat for Cinderella's father
- Corrugated card
- Gold and silver glitter
- An old high-heeled shoe, preferably small adult-size (from a charity shop)
- Gold metallic paint
- A cushion to carry the 'glass slipper' on
- Balloons
- A parachute for parachute games
- Broom (if possible like a witch's)
- Broom handle

# The fairy tale castle

## Personal, Social and Emotional Development

 *Work as part of a group, taking turns and sharing fairly.*

### Circle time

- Talk about taking turns in the role play area. Ask: What do we do to make it fair? How do we give everyone a turn? Tell the children that you have an older sister. Tell them that when you were young your sister was always allowed to choose first. Was this fair? How could this have been made fairer?
- Read the poem 'Favouritism' (see page 33). Discuss this with the class. Ask: Was it really favouritism? Why do you think the author thought it was unfair?
- Remind them about Cinderella's ugly sisters and her stepmother. Ask: Did they treat Cinderella fairly? What do you think of the ugly sisters? Would you like to be treated like Cinderella, having to do all the work while her sisters did nothing? Can you think of some words to describe Cinderella's sisters?

## Mathematical Development

 *Say and use number names in familiar contexts.*

### Telling the time

- Look at a clock. Count the numbers from 1 to 12. Show the children how to form the numbers. Ask them to show you by drawing the numbers in the air with the index finger of their writing hand. Then ask the children to write the numbers in the sand tray. When you are happy with the formation, let them write the numbers very large on sheets of paper, using very thin paint. Finally, ask them to write them on whiteboards.
- Talk about telling the time. Ask: What do we call 12 o'clock at night/in the middle of the day?
- Make available a clock with moveable hands. Talk about the hour and minute hands. Remind the children that Cinderella had to be home by midnight. Ask them to show you midnight on the clock. Show the children how to show, for example, 6 o'clock. Can they think of something they do or that happens at 6 o'clock in the evening?

**Extension**

- Show the children how to play a clock game, for two players. You will need a clock with moveable hands, one or two dice and a pile of counters. Place the pile of counters and a dice in the middle of the table. Child A rolls the dice. If, for example, he throws 3, he shows 3 o'clock on the clock. If he does it correctly, he takes a counter. If he can tell you something that happens at 3 o'clock, he takes another counter. Then Child B throws the dice and so on. The winner is the first to get ten counters. (To make it even more challenging, ask the players to use two dice.)

### Subtraction

- Play 'Kim's game' with 12 items. Place 12 small items on a tray. Ask the children to identify and count them. Cover the tray with a cloth. Tell the children to shut their eyes while you remove one item. Who can be first to tell you which item is missing? Ask the children how many items are left – count with them. Repeat, but remove two or more items. Again, ask how many are left.

## Communication, Language and Literacy

 *Sustain attentive listening, responding to what they have heard with relevant comments, questions or actions.*

### Listening

- Read a version of the story of Cinderella (see Resources). Talk about the story and encourage the children to make comments on how the different characters behave.
- Say the poem 'Cinderella Rockerfella' (page 33) and ask the children to join in. Perform the poem for an assembly.

### Video

- Show the children excerpts of the *Cinderella* video (see Resources). Talk about things that are the same as the book version and things that are different.

# The fairy tale castle

### Writing: teacher modelling

- Talk about invitations and explain that you are going to write an invitation to the ball. Talk about making the reason for the invitation clear and discuss the different ways that you could write the heading – capital letters, writing in a different colour and so on.
- Explain that you must tell people where the ball will be held and the day and time. Write:

> Please come to a ball
> on Friday
> at The King's Palace
> Time: 8·00pm to 1·00am

Talk about the writing process, leaving spaces between words, using capital letters and so on.

### Writing: independent

- Place small pieces of card and writing materials in a box on the table. Encourage the children to write their own invitations to the ball when in role in the castle. Provide some glue and glitter somewhere in the classroom. Show the children how, when they have writtten an invitation, they can decorate it. Put a line of glue all around the edge of the invitation and sprinkle glitter over. Shake the card to remove excess glitter and allow to dry thoroughly.

#### Extension

- Help the children to write a letter accepting the invitation. Tell them to mention what they are invited to and when it is, to say they are happy to go to the ball and to sign their names.

### Music and song

- Sing 'What's she doing?' from *Bingo Lingo* (see Resources).

## Knowledge and Understanding of the World

 *Find out about past and present events.*

### Clocks

- Talk with the children about the different types of clocks. Show them examples or pictures, if possible.
- Ask: Why do we need clocks? Talk about ways people told the time before clocks – show them an egg timer. Talk about people going to bed as soon as it was dark and rising when it was light. Talk about sundials and how the hours were marked using the sun.
- Show the children an example of an alarm clock and set it for 12 o'clock (a few minutes ahead, to go off during the discussion). You could make a collection of alarm clocks.
- Sing 'Hickory digital clock' from *Tom Thumb's Musical Maths* (see Resources).

### Dances: now and then

- Show the class the ballroom scene from the video of *Cinderella* (see Resources).
- Talk about dances and balls. Discuss what people wore then, how Cinderella got to the dance and what kind of dances they danced. Ask the children what dances they think Cinderella would go to if she lived today. Ask: What would she wear? How would she get to the dance? What kind of dancing would she do?

**Starting** *with role play – Fairy tales*

# The fairy tale castle

> ### Creative Development
>
> *Explore colour, shape, texture, form and space in two or three dimensions.*

### Fairy tale castle

- First, remove the giant's castle, all props and the background from the role play area. Create the background for the inside of the fairy tale castle (see page 35). Ask the children to help you make the following as appropriate: a chandelier, a candelabra, the pumpkin, the mice, the slipper, the horses' headbands, the coach, the fireplace and the clock (see pages 35–37).

### Music and song

- Sing 'Cinderella' from *Three Tapping Teddies* (see Resources).

> ### Physical Development
>
> *Use a range of small and large equipment.*

### Dancing

- Remind the children of the ball scene. Explain that they are going to learn to dance a waltz. Tell them to find a partner. Show them how to bow and curtsey to each other. Ask them to hold inside hands and show them how to walk with one long and then two short steps. Ask them to count in threes as they move. Play suitable waltz music – for example, *The Blue Danube* slowed down a little.

### Outside

- The prince and Cinderella married 'and lived happily ever after'. After the wedding everyone celebrated. They were treated to a spectacular firework display. Explain that the children are going to recreate the firework display with balloons and a parachute.
- Lay the parachute flat on the ground. Ask the children to stand all around the edge. Practise waving the parachute, gently at first, then getting faster and faster. Slow movements down and return the parachute to the ground.
- Raise the parachute and throw a balloon into the middle. Ask the children to see how quickly they can make the balloon bounce off. Try making big, slow movements and quick, jerky movements.
- Next, throw lots of balloons into the middle. Ask the children to see how high they can make them bounce. Can they keep them on the parachute and bounce them high, just like fireworks? (Try this activity with large and small balls and compare height and ease of keeping them on the parachute to that of the balloons.)

# Fairy tales

## WEEK 6

### The role play area

During this week the children will use the role play area to re-enact the story of Cinderella. A long table will be set for a banquet. The children will make **crowns** and **junk model castles**. At the end of the unit they will attend a ball and dance to different styles of music there.

### Resources

Photocopiable:

Poems and rhymes 1 and 2 (pages 32 and 33)

Fiction books:

*I Want my Dinner!* by Tony Ross, Picture Lions (0 006643 56 6)
*Once Upon a Time* by John Prater, Walker (0 744536 90 1)
*Whose House?* by Colin and Jacqui Hawkins, Collins (0 001007 41 6)
*One, Two, Guess Who?* by Colin and Jacqui Hawkins, Collins (0 001361 18 X)
*Each Peach Pear Plum* by Janet and Allan Ahlberg, Puffin (0 140509 19 4)

Non fiction book:

*How Should I Behave?* by Mick Manning and Brita Granstrom, Franklin Watts (0 749639 98 9)

Materials:

- Long table or two smaller ones put together
- Tablecloth
- Plates, bowls, mugs and plastic food for the banqueting table
- Paper plates
- Food for a banquet – jelly, sandwiches with jam and honey, cocktail sausages
- Music – waltzes, jazz, pop

Ask the children to bring in a few biscuits, pieces of fruit and crisps or other savouries for the banquet at the end of the week. It is best to send a short note home to the parents/carers, giving ideas and quantities of items to be sent in.

# The banquet

## Personal, Social and Emotional Development

 *Form good relations with adults and peers.*

### Discussion

- Talk about the ball. Explain that it was a special party given by the prince. Ask: Have you been to a party? What were you celebrating? What did you do? Did you have a good time? What did you like best? What food/drink did you have? Invite all the children to contribute by taking turns to speak round the circle. Ask: What do you think the guests did at the prince's ball? Did they have party food? What sorts of things were on the table for the guests to eat? Tell them that they are going to celebrate the wedding of Cinderella and the prince with a special banquet at the end of the week.
- Share a book about good manners, such as *I Want my Dinner* (see Resources). People give food and gifts at parties. Talk about how we should say 'Please' and 'Thank you'. Ask the children if they think that princesses have to have good manners. Work in pairs; ask them to role play being Cinderella, the prince, the king or the queen. They should offer their partner some gifts. How would they respond? Ask one or two children to come and perform their conversation to the rest of the group.

## Mathematical Development

 *Use language such as 'smaller' to compare sizes.*

### Size

- Talk about how the glass slipper would only fit Cinderella. She had the smallest feet.
- Draw round children's feet and ask them to cut them out. Discuss ways of finding out who has the tiniest feet. Remind them how they measured footprints when they were looking at the story of Jack and the Beanstalk.
- Put the children into small groups. Give each group a set of small objects to fill their 'feet'. Ask: Who has the tiniest feet in your group? Compare the tiniest from each group to find the tiniest of all.

### Positional language

- Using the coach and mice (see Creative Development, week 5), ask the children to stand in front of the coach, behind the coach, and at the side of the coach. Ask them to position the mice above, below, behind, between, against and so on.

### Counting

- Read the poem 'A bedtime rhyme for young fairies' (see page 32) and talk about the counting words.

**Extension**

- As you read the poem again, ask the children to write the number you say on their whiteboards.

## Communication, Language and Literacy

 *Enjoy listening to and using spoken and written language and readily turn to it in their role play.*

### Listening

- Share with groups of children one of the books that makes reference to other traditional fairy tales and characters (see Resources). Ask them how many stories they recognise.

### Syllables

- Sit the children in a circle. Ask them to take it in turns to tap the syllables in the names of the main characters from this unit – for example, Cin/der/ell/a; gi/ant; ug/ly sis/ter.

### Rhythm tapping game

- In the castle, sit the children in a circle. Practise tapping knees to a regular beat. When they can keep the beat, explain that they are going to miss out the third tap and say something they can see in the castle – for example, 'Tap, tap, pumpkin. Tap, tap, chair.'

# The banquet

### Writing: poem

- Read the poem 'The new fairy godmother' (see page 32). Encourage the children to join in. Talk about the poem with them and explain that they are going to help you write a poem of wishes. Tell them that poems do not have to rhyme but they need a rhythm. Say that the poem is going to start 'Close your eyes and make a wish, Wish for something special. 'Ask three children to complete the line 'I wish I had a …' Then repeat the refrain.
- Write down the children's suggestions on the board. Explain that you will edit the poem so that it has a good rhythm. Type out the poem in large print and display it in the classroom. Some children might like to illustrate the poem round the border.

#### Extension

- Ask the children to work with a partner to write their own wish poems. Write the refrain for them and ask them to complete the lists of three wishes.

> ## Knowledge and Understanding of the World
>  *Ask questions about why things happen and how things change.*

### Party food

- In small groups, working with an adult helper, make some food for the banquet. Make a jelly. Talk about melting and setting. Make jam or honey sandwiches. Cook cocktail sausages. Talk about why we need to cook meat thoroughly.

> ## Creative Development
>  *Express and communicate their ideas through designing and making songs.*

### Laying the table

- Ask the children to set the banqueting table with plates, pretend food and so on to use in their role play.

### Making crowns

- When Cinderella married the prince she became a princess. Tell the children that they are going to make a crown to wear at the banquet. They can choose to be either the prince or the princess. Cut strips of card and ask the children to decorate them. Provide a selection of shiny paper, glitter, tissue scraps and some glue sticks. Staple the bands to fit.

### Junk models

- Make junk model castles. Provide a selection of boxes, card and collage materials. Ask pairs of children to make fairy tale castles.
- Build fairy tale castles with construction kits.

### Music

- On the day of the banquet, play a variety of musical styles in the castle – for example, Strauss waltzes, Scott Joplin jazz and current pop music. Let the children experiment with dancing and moving to the different styles (keep the groups in the castle small!)

> ## Physical Development
>  *Move with confidence, imagination and control.*

### Movement

- Use the music (see Creative Development) for party games on the day of the banquet – for example; musical statues, musical bumps, musical chairs and pass the parcel.
- Do the hokey cokey!
- Enjoy the banquet!

### Review and evaluation

*Encourage the children to reflect on the topic. What have they enjoyed learning about? Which part has been most exciting? Which stories and poems do they remember? Which activity did they most enjoy doing? Would they like to be a prince, princess or giant?*

# Dwarf and equipment

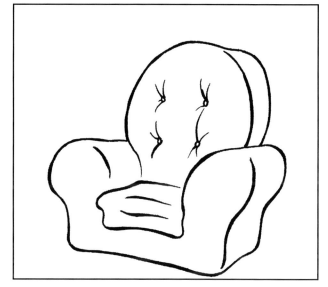

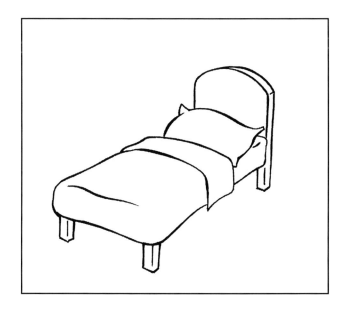

**Starting** with role play

# Poems and rhymes 1

**The digging song**
In your hands you hold the spade,
Feel its well worn wood.
Now you drive it in the earth,
Drive it deep and good.

Dig dig digging dirt
Dirt inside your vest.
Dig dig digging dirt,
Digging dirt is best.

Soon your hands are red and raw,
Blisters on the way,
But your spade just wants to dig
All the long hot day.

Dig dig digging dirt…

Wes Magee

**Run, Jack, run**
(Sing to the tune of *Three blind mice*)

Run, Jack, run.
Run, Jack, run.
The giant's getting closer,
The giant's getting closer.
Run, Jack, run.

Quick, Jack, quick.
The giant has a great big stick.

Climb, Jack, climb.
The giant's right behind you.

Maggie Hutchings

**A bedtime rhyme for young fairies**
One tired fairy,
Two folded wings,
Three magic wishes,
Four daisy rings,
Five moonlight dancers,
Six starlight spells,
Seven hidden treasures,
Eight silver bells,
Nine secret doorways,
Ten keys to keep,
And one little fairy
Fast asleep.

Clare Bevan

**The new fairy godmother**
The new fairy godmother's having fun,
Casting spells for EVERYONE.

The giant has a teddy bear
Extra big.
The wolf has a cosy house
Built for a pig.
The princess is married to
A handsome frog.
The three blind mice
Have a helpful dog.
The witch has a speedboat.
Her cat has new boots.
The duck and the penguin
Have diving suits.
The rabbit has a roar.
The fish has a bark.
The mole has a torch
To shine in the dark.
The cow has a rocket.
The spoon has a dish.
And you? Close your eyes.
Make your own, special wish.

The new fairy godmother's having fun,
Casting spells for EVERYONE.

Clare Bevan

## Poems and rhymes 2

**I'd be a good friend**

Everyone's a friend of someone
Although it seems to be
That every friend has got a friend
Who's not a friend to me.

I'd be a good friend to someone
Fun to be with, and kind.
I'd be as happy as an eight-armed goalie
As sweet as a jam roly poly
As cool as a knickerbocker glory
As warm as a bedtime story
If only a friend I could find.

Roger McGough

**Giant's breakfast – a counting rhyme**

I WANT
ONE sack of sugar on my teaspoon,
TWO jugs of milk in my tea;
THREE bags of tea-leaves in the teapot –
and don't forget to STIR it well for me!

I WANT
FOUR packs of porridge made with cream now,
FIVE tins of treacle stirred well in;
SIX big bananas chopped on top, please –
I don't want to end up looking THIN!

I WANT
SEVEN loaves of bread on my plate, please,
EIGHT jars of jam just for me;
NINE trays of bacon, egg and sausage –
I'm not greedy in the morning, as you see!

Judith Nicholls

**Favouritism**

When we caught measles
It wasn't fair –
My brother collected
Twice his share.

He counted my spots:
'One hundred and twenty!'
Which sounded to me
As if I had plenty.
Then I counted his –
And what do you think?
He'd two hundred and thirty-eight,
Small, round and pink!

I felt I'd been cheated
So 'Count mine again!'
I told him, and scowled
So he dare not complain.

'One hundred and twenty' –
The same as before …
In our house, he's youngest
And he always gets more!

Trevor Harvey

**Cinderella Rockerfella**

Cinderella Rockerfella 1, 2, 3
How many white mice did she see?
Cinderella Rockerfella 4, 5, 6
How many footmen playing tricks?
Cinderella Rockerfella 7, 8, 9
How many grand guests sitting down to dine?
Cinderella Rockerfella, oh dear, oh dear,
The chimes of the palace clock, I hear
1, 2, 3, 4, 5, 6, 7, 8, 9, 10, 11, 12
*(getting louder)*

Dee Reid

## Puppets and beanstalk

### Wooden spoon puppets

You will need
- wooden spoons
- google eyes
- paints
- felt
- fabric scraps

1. Ask the children to work in pairs.
2. Give each pair a character from the story and tell them that they are going to make a puppet on a spoon.
3. Paint the head with a skin tone.
4. Add features such as google eyes, wool hair, felt rosy cheeks and a mouth.
5. Make clothes cut out of felt (two layers and glued over the stick) or lengths of fabric fixed with an elastic band.
6. Cut some hands out of felt and glue them on.

### The class beanstalk

You will need
- a container such as a large coffee tin with a hole drilled in the lid
- garden twine
- ring, fixed to ceiling or high on a wall
- sand
- green crepe paper

1. Remove the lid from the tin, thread the end of the twine through the hole and tape firmly to the base of the tin. Fill the tin with sand and replace lid. Tape the lid down.
2. Unroll the twine. You will need three times the distance from the tin to the ceiling. This will allow the beanstalk to 'grow' and also to fall back into the pot. Feed the twine through the ring.
3. Glue or tape crepe paper leaves to the twine for the length of the twine from pot to ceiling (ie one third of its length).
4. When the beanstalk is fully 'grown', tie the end of the twine to a fixture such as a coat hook or a pipe.
5. Place the base (tin filled with sand) in a box so that the beanstalk is protected when down.

### Individual beanstalks

You will need
- a small container (yogurt pot) for each child
- string
- green tissue paper
- threading beads, larger than the rings
- white fabric such as sheeting
- dowel rods
- plaster of Paris
- net curtain rings (eyes)
- glue sticks

*The children will need plenty of adult support to assemble their beanstalk. Prepare everything beforehand as you will have to work quickly. Take groups of four children at a time.*

1. Cut a length of string twice the length of the dowel rod, plus 15cm. Tell the children to cut their own lengths by matching an example.
2. Tie or tape one end of the string firmly to the bottom of the rod.
3. Screw a ring into the top.
4. Mix the plaster of Paris with water to a thick, pouring consistency.
5. Pour into the pot, almost to the top.
6. Insert the bottom of the rod, with the string attached, into the pot as far as it will go (make sure you hold the rest of the string above the surface).
7. Allow to dry and harden thoroughly. Paint the surface of the plaster green.
8. Cut tissue leaves and glue along the string from the base to the top of the rod.
9. Thread the string through the eye.
10. Thread and tie a bead to the end of the string to prevent it slipping through. Gently pull the string and watch your beanstalk grow.

# The inside of the palace 1

### Classroom background

You will need
- white backing paper to line the walls
- deep blue paint
- silver stars or silver paint
- purple fabric or crepe paper
- grey sugar paper
- pink and lilac paint
- pale grey paint
- gold metallic paint
- sponges
- corrugated card

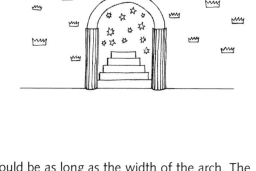

1. Draw an arch slightly above child height.
2. Sponge paint in pink and lilac all over the paper except under the arch. When dry, using gold paint and a small brush, paint tiny crowns randomly over the pink and lilac.
3. Next, carefully sponge paint under the arch in deep blue, to represent the night sky.
4. Add stars, either stuck on or painted with a very small brush.
5. Make steps by cutting strips of grey sugar paper. The first strip should be as long as the width of the arch. The second strip should be shorter, the third shorter still. You will probably need to cut about six steps.
6. Starting with pale grey paint and the longest step, sponge stone shapes with a large piece of sponge. Gradually make the paint darker as the steps get smaller. Try to make the last step almost the same colour as the sky by adding some of the blue paint. Glue the steps, in order, under the arch.
7. With thick gold paint, paint a frame around the top of the arch.
8. Line the role play area with the backing paper.
9. Cut two lengths of corrugated card, to reach from the floor to the base of the curve of the arch, and paint them gold. Fix these on either side of the arch as pillars. If you can curve them, the effect will be 3-D.
10. Take the purple fabric and drape swathes across the background at ceiling level. If you do not have fabric try using crepe paper.

### Chandelier

You will need
- a small hula hoop
- foil wrap
- string
- a few beads

1. Tie six lengths of string to the hoop at regular intervals. Tie the ends together. This is to suspend the chandelier from the ceiling.
2. Tie several short lengths of string (they do not have to be the same length) around the hoop to hang.
3. Wind strips of foil to cover the hoop.
4. Cut circles of foil for lights. Using glue sticks, stick pairs of circles onto the strings. String should be enclosed through the foil circles.
5. Cover beads with foil (scrunch it over the beads), push a stout needle through to reveal the holes and thread to the bottom of each length of string.
6. Suspend the chandelier from the ceiling inside the castle.

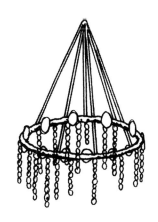

**Starting** with role play

## The inside of the palace 2

### Candelabra

You will need
- a silver cake board or circle of card covered with foil
- lengths of cardboard tube (about 10cm)
- foil wrap and yellow card

1. Cover each tube with foil.
2. Snip into one end of each tube. Flatten the bottom and stick with PVA glue round the board.
3. Cut flame shapes out of yellow card. The base of the flames should be a little wider than the diameter of the tubes. Cut two slits in the base of the flames so that they can be slotted onto the top of the tubes.
4. Glue twists of foil around the base of each tube to decorate. Place the candelabra on the table.

### Pumpkin

You will need
- A3 card
- orange and brown paint

1. Draw a large pumpkin on A3 card.
2. Paint it on both sides in orange and brown.
3. Laminate.

### Mice

You will need
- thin card
- hole punch
- grey or brown paint
- brown or grey pipe-cleaners

1. Ask the children to draw, cut out and paint mice.
2. Laminate.
3. Punch a hole in the bottom of each mouse and add a grey or brown pipe-cleaner tail.

### Slipper

You will need
- a shoe
- PVA glue
- silver glitter

Cover the outside of the shoe with PVA glue and sprinkle silver glitter over. Allow to dry thoroughly.

### Horses' headbands

You will need
- strips of card
- feathers
- sticky tape

1. Make three or four headbands for the horses.
2. Cut and staple strips of card to make bands and tape a few feathers to the front.

## The inside of the palace 3

### Clock

You will need
- paper plate
- permanent marker and gold paint
- black card or paper

1. Paint the plate gold.
2. Write the numbers round the clock with a permanent marker.
3. Make hands cut from black paper or card and glue to the clock face to show 12 o'clock.
4. Stick or staple to the wall inside the castle.

### Fireplace

You will need
- brown paper
- black card
- light sticks or twigs
- orange and red crepe paper

1. On a background of brown paper, stick twigs to represent the fire.
2. Cut flames out of orange and red crepe paper and stick them onto the fire.
3. Draw and cut out of black card a cooking pot to sit on the fire.
4. Fix this to a wall inside the castle.
5. Put a broom near the fireplace.

### Coach

You will need
- large sheets of rigid card (shop display boards would be ideal)
- a broom handle
- gold metallic paint
- shiny collage materials

1. Draw and cut out the main body of the coach
2. Cut out a window towards the top. (You may need to use a craft knife as the board could be very thick. Do this well away from the children.)
3. Paint with gold metallic paint and decorate with jewels (cut from scraps of shiny paper, sequins or blobs of coloured glitter).
4. Mark the door with a black permanent marker.
5. Cut two wheels out of rigid card and paint half gold and half black.
6. Paint a gold rim all the way round. Glue on strips of gold foil for the spokes.
7. Firmly fix the wheels to the carriage, with the black half below the body (see picture).
8. Use PVA glue and/or double-sided tape and reinforce with parcel tape at the back.
9. Just below the window at the back, firmly tape the broom handle to the carriage.
10. The footmen can carry the carriage while Cinderella walks behind, face visible through the window!

**Starting** with role play

# Observational Assessment Chart

Unit: _____  Class: _____  Date: _____

| Name | Personal, Social and Emotional Development | Communication, Language and Literacy | Knowledge & Understanding of the World | Mathematical Development | Creative Development | Physical Development |
|---|---|---|---|---|---|---|
| | Y B G ELG | Y B G ELG | Y B G ELG | Y B G ELG | Y B G ELG | Y B G ELG |
| | Y B G ELG | Y B G ELG | Y B G ELG | Y B G ELG | Y B G ELG | Y B G ELG |
| | Y B G ELG | Y B G ELG | Y B G ELG | Y B G ELG | Y B G ELG | Y B G ELG |
| | Y B G ELG | Y B G ELG | Y B G ELG | Y B G ELG | Y B G ELG | Y B G ELG |
| | Y B G ELG | Y B G ELG | Y B G ELG | Y B G ELG | Y B G ELG | Y B G ELG |
| | Y B G ELG | Y B G ELG | Y B G ELG | Y B G ELG | Y B G ELG | Y B G ELG |
| | Y B G ELG | Y B G ELG | Y B G ELG | Y B G ELG | Y B G ELG | Y B G ELG |
| | Y B G ELG | Y B G ELG | Y B G ELG | Y B G ELG | Y B G ELG | Y B G ELG |
| | Y B G ELG | Y B G ELG | Y B G ELG | Y B G ELG | Y B G ELG | Y B G ELG |
| | Y B G ELG | Y B G ELG | Y B G ELG | Y B G ELG | Y B G ELG | Y B G ELG |
| | Y B G ELG | Y B G ELG | Y B G ELG | Y B G ELG | Y B G ELG | Y B G ELG |
| | Y B G ELG | Y B G ELG | Y B G ELG | Y B G ELG | Y B G ELG | Y B G ELG |
| | Y B G ELG | Y B G ELG | Y B G ELG | Y B G ELG | Y B G ELG | Y B G ELG |
| | Y B G ELG | Y B G ELG | Y B G ELG | Y B G ELG | Y B G ELG | Y B G ELG |
| | Y B G ELG | Y B G ELG | Y B G ELG | Y B G ELG | Y B G ELG | Y B G ELG |

Circle the relevant Stepping Stones (Y = Yellow; B = Blue; G = Green or ELG = Early Learning Goal) and write a positive comment as evidence of achievement.

**Starting** with role play